OLYMPIC JOKES

THE CHILD'S WORLD

Library of Congress Catalog-in-Publication Data
Rothaus, James R.
Olympic Jokes / Jim Rothaus
p. cm.
Summary: Presents a collection of riddle, jokes, and
knock-knocks about Olympic athletes, coaches, and events.
ISBN 1-56766-270-6 (Lib. Bdg.)

1. Riddles, Juvenile. 2. Knock-knock jokes. 3. Sports — Juvenile
humor. 4. Olympics — Juvenile humor. [1. Riddles. 2. Jokes.
3. Knock-knocks jokes . 4. Olympics — Wit and humor.
5. Athletes — Wit and humor. 6. Sports — Wit and humor.]
I. Title
PN6371.5R679 1997   95-47111
818'.5402 — dc20   CIP
[B]   AC

OLYMPIC
JOKES

Written and Compiled by James R. Rothaus
Illustrated by Viki Woodworth

Why can't a tennis shoe talk?

Because it is tongue-tied. ⇨

Did you hear about the athlete who never learned to swim?
He couldn't keep his mouth closed long enough.

Knock-knock.
Who's there?
Heart.
Heart who?
Heart to see the game very well from here.

What do Winter Olympians have when there is no snow?
Tough sledding.

Knock-knock.
Who's there?
Aldo.
Aldo who?
Aldo my best, you do the rest.

What did one bicycle wheel say to the other?
Was it you who just spoke?

How are judges like basketball referees?

They both work the courts. ⟵

What does Olympic star Greg Luganis do on Friday nights?
He goes to a dive in movie.

Knock-knock.
Who's there?
Wendy.
Wendy who?
Wendy games are over, let's get together.

What did the athlete's sock say to the foot?
Your putting me on.

Knock-knock.
Who's there?
Dennis.
Dennis who?
Dennis anyone?

Why was he considered the cream of prize fighters?
He always got whipped.

What does an Olympic boxer drink?
Punch. ⇨

How does a flea get from one athlete to another?
By itch-hiking.

Knock-knock.
Who's there?
Scott.
Scott who?
Scott nothing to do with Olympics.

What is the best way to win a race?
Run faster than anyone else.

Knock-knock.
Who's there?
Atlas.
Atlas who?
Atlas I've won an Olympic medal.

What is the difference between an Olympic boxing champion and a man with a cold?
One knows his blows and the other blows his nose.

When is an athlete like a dog?

When he is a boxer. ⟵

How do they take underwater pictures in the Olympics?
They use splash cubes.

Knock-knock.
Who's there?
Disk.
Disk who?
Disk in case we should lose.

Why are swimmers patient?
Because they are used to wading.

Knock-knock.
Who's there?
Police.
Police who?
Police let me know who won the race.

What can you serve but never eat?
A tennis ball.

Why should an Olympic swimmer never swim on an empty stomach?
Because it's much easier to swim in water. ⇨

What do they call an Olympic bicycle rider who is constantly in training?
A cycle-path.

Knock-knock.
Who's there?
Elsie.
Elsie who?
Elsie you in the locker room.

Why did the athlete choose to be a wrestler?
It was a sport that really grabbed him.

Knock-knock.
Who's there?
Omaha.
Omaha who?
Omaha goodness, can that guy run!

Why do Olympians choose to play soccer?
They get a kick out of it.

What is an Olympic figure skater's favorite number?

The figure 8. ⇦

What's one food all runners should eat?
Ketchup.

Knock-knock.
Who's there?
Chason.
Chason who?
Chason the guy with the baton.

Ski Coach: *Jackie, I wish you would pay a little attention.*
Jackie: *I'm paying as little as possible.*

Knock-knock.
Who's there?
Sid.
Sid who?
Sid any where you want, coach.

Olympic Coach: *Why did you miss practice yesterday?*
Athlete: *I was sick.*
Coach: *Sick of what?*
Athlete: *Sick of practice.*

What is the hardest thing about learning to figure skate?
The ice. ⇨

Olympic Trainer: *Look at this chart. You're over weight.*
Athlete: *No, I'm not. I'm just six inches too short.*

Knock-knock.
Who's there?
Abbott.
Abbott who?
Abbott my friend George wins a medal.

How did the Olympic athlete cure his sleepwalking?
By scattering thumbtacks on his bedroom floor.

Knock-knock.
Who's there?
Justin.
Justin who?
Justin time for the last race.

Why did the Olympic athlete throw his alarm clock out the window?
He wanted to see time fly.

What is a cow's favorite Olympic event?
Herdles. ⇦

If athletes suffer from athlete's feet, what do astronauts suffer from?
Mistletoe.

Knock-knock.
Who's there?
Thistle.
Thistle who?
Thistle be the last event of the day.

How do you like being an Olympic ski jumper?
It has it's ups and downs.

Knock-knock.
Who's there?
Harmony.
Harmony who?
Harmony times will you win the game?

Any kid could be an Olympic basketball star when he grows up and up and up.

Why did the Olympic athlete take a ruler to bed with him?
So he could see how long he slept. ⇨

A good boxer is one who's learned it's better to give than receive.

Knock-knock.
Who's there?
Alaska.
Alaska who?
Alaska the coach.

What do they call a beat up Olympic boxer?
A sore loser.

Knock-knock.
Who's there?
Needle.
Needle who?
Needle little time to warm up.

Olympic athlete: *Dad, what would you do if you were in my shoes?*
Dad: *Polish them.*

Why did the marathon runner go to the veterinarian?

Because his calves hurt. ⟵

What would you call an Olympic jacket that goes up in flame?
A blazer.

Knock-knock.
Who's there?
Norma Lee.
Norma Lee who?
Norma Lee we win more than we lose.

Knock-knock.
Who's there?
Diesel.
Diesel who?
Diesel fit me just fine.

Knock-knock.
Who's there?
Formosa.
Formosa who?
Formosa the time he was leading the race.